Bishop's Lydeard, Somerset: a sixteenth-century bench end of a post mill, with the miller and a packhorse in the foreground.

CHURCH MISERICORDS AND BENCH ENDS

Richard Hayman

Shire Publications Ltd

CONTENTS

Printed in Great Britain by C. I. Thomas & Sons (Haverfordwest) Ltd, Press Buildings, Merlins Bridge, Haverfordwest, Dyfed SA61 1XF.

British Library Cataloguing in Publication Data: Hayman, Richard. Church misericords and bench ends. 1 Great Britain. Churches. Benches. Misericords. Wood carvings. I. Title. 729'. 93. ISBN 0-85263-996-1.

ACKNOWLEDGEMENTS
Permission to reproduce photographs has been given by the Dean and Chapter of Carlisle, Ely, Exeter, Lincoln, Norwich, Ripon, Winchester and Worcester Cathedrals and the Dean and Canons of Manchester Cathedral and St George's Chapel, Windsor Castle. The author would also like to thank Mr B. Perry at Cartmel Priory, Steve Mitchell, Julia Hayman and Martin and Deborah Gillham.

Cover: *The choir stalls at Beverley Minster, Humberside, with a seat tipped up to reveal the misericord.*

Below: *Great Malvern Priory, Worcestershire: a misericord showing a monk driving away a demon using a pair of bellows applied to the demon's rectum.*

Ludlow, Shropshire: misericord: an owl, representing the Jew, being mobbed by two smaller birds to the left and right.

INTRODUCTION

At Ludlow in Shropshire there is a carving on a fifteenth-century misericord of an owl. Traditionally the owl is a symbol of wisdom, but in the medieval world it meant the exact opposite — ignorance and, more specifically, the Jew who preferred darkness to the light of Christianity. On either side of the owl are smaller birds which are intended to be mobbing it, thus representing the sinner under attack from the righteous, a scene also found on a misericord at Norwich Cathedral.

The meaning in this carving would have been apparent to all those who saw it and this is just one example of the illustrated stories that were used to convey the message of the Christian faith in the middle ages. Indeed, at a time when the populace was illiterate, sermons were few and the Mass was said in Latin, visual art was one of the most effective forms of communication.

In comparison to stained glass, sculpture and wall paintings, misericords and bench ends were considered minor art forms, partly because they were carved out of wood rather than stone. Misericords were hidden beneath the seats of the choir stalls and could be seen only by the clergy who used them. Bench ends,

because they were prominently displayed inside parish churches, served more of a didactic function. Nevertheless, they were still considered to be of minor status and would certainly have had less impact than the stained glass figures of saints and the Day of Judgement scene painted on the east wall of the nave. However, this minor status allowed the carvers a greater freedom of expression than was possible elsewhere inside the church, a freedom which resulted, especially on misericords, in a large number of carvings of secular subjects alongside the usual religious themes.

Ironically, it is largely because these woodcarvings were considered to be of marginal importance that so many of them have survived. Now that most of the stained glass, sculpture and painting has vanished from Britain's churches (most of it destroyed) misericords and bench ends have an increased importance in giving us an insight into the medieval mind — its spiritualism, moralising and wit — as well as giving us a picture of everyday life in the middle ages. Furthermore, their distribution is so widespread that they can be found in almost any place of worship, from the grandest cathedral to the smallest parish church.

MISERICORDS

The seats in medieval choir stalls were hinged so that when tipped up they revealed a ledge supported by a corbel. The corbel is known as a misericord, a word derived from the Latin *misericordia* (meaning pity) and alluding to the original function of the ledge. The rule of St Benedict, introduced in the sixth century AD, required the monks to sing the daily offices of the Church — Matins, Lauds, Prime, Terce, Sext, Nones, Vespers and Compline — standing up. Only for the Epistle and Gradual at Mass and the Response at Vespers were they able to sit. Older monks soon adopted a leaning staff or crutch to help take the weight off

Kidlington, Oxfordshire: bench end: a kid, a ling and a ton. This representation of a name by a series of pictures is called a rebus and was usually applied to people rather than places.

their feet during the long hours they spent in the choir stalls. By the eleventh century, despite protests from the more strict disciplinarians, a slight relaxation in the rules was allowed and the misericord was introduced to enable the monks to lean back against a ledge for greater comfort, whilst at the same time giving the appearance of standing up straight.

The earliest mention of misericords appears in the eleventh century in the rules of the monastery at Hirsau in Germany. They were attached to the upper rows of the choir stalls and reserved for the use of the older monks. We do not know when misericords were first introduced into Britain but the earliest surviving examples are at Hemingbrough in North Yorkshire and Christchurch in Dorset and date from the early thirteenth century. The earliest complete set is in Exeter Cathedral and dates from the years 1240 to 1270.

Misericords were in use in the cathedral, abbey and collegiate churches, where the monks or canons were required to sing the daily offices. Sometimes they appeared in parish churches as well, but only when the church accommodated a special college of priests or, in rare cases, when a small outlying cell of a monastery shared its church with the local parish. The priests in parish churches did not require misericords for the saying of the Mass and they sat on stone seats known as sedilia.

The choir seat, the ledge and the corbel supporting it were fashioned from a single piece of wood, usually oak. Medieval craftsmen had an aversion to bare surfaces and they must very quickly have seized the opportunity to carve scenes on the underside of the ledge. The word misericord is now taken to refer to the carving rather than the ledge itself. British misericords differ from those on the continent of Europe in that they have subsidiary carvings, known as supporters, on either side of the centrally carved scene. This gave the carver scope to develop the theme of the central carving if he so wished. These supporters, like the central carving itself,

4

Exeter Cathedral: a mid thirteenth-century misericord showing the Swan Knight, legendary hero of the First Crusade.

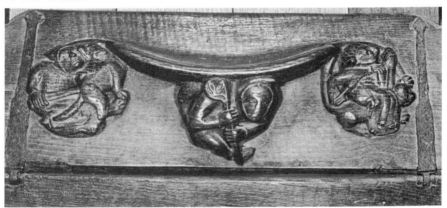

Winchester Cathedral: in this early fourteenth-century misericord the supporters, a witch riding a cat on the right and a man fighting the cat on the left, are given equal significance to the central carving of a mock bishop.

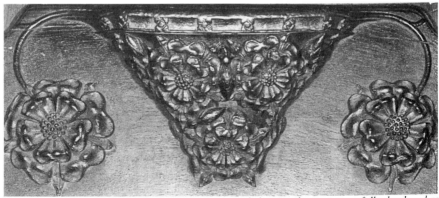

Lincoln Cathedral: a late fourteenth-century misericord showing the supporters fully developed as wing carvings. Nearly half of Britain's misericords are of foliage.

5

Above: *Tong, Shropshire: a typical medieval choir stall with its misericord, a moulded back and angels carved on the arm rests.*

Left: *Manchester Cathedral: the choir stalls here were constructed between 1485 and 1506. The lavishly decorated stall end has the arms of Richard Beswick, a prosperous Manchester merchant.*

became more exuberant as the carvers became more confident of their subject matter. However, the carvers did not confine their efforts solely to the misericords. The choir stalls had beautifully moulded backs, with figure carvings on the arm rests. Above the seats were canopies and the stall ends were enriched in the manner of church bench ends.

6

Left: *Down St Mary, Devon: a typical square-headed West Country bench end, dating from the sixteenth century and decorated with foliage and panelling.*

Right: *Dennington, Suffolk: most of the East Anglian bench ends have a finial, or poppy-head, with a carving on the arm rest.*

BENCH ENDS

Like the monks, medieval congregations in parish churches were obliged to stand for the duration of the Mass. The nave of the church was used for secular as well as religious purposes and this precluded the introduction of seating on a large scale until these secular practices were moved outside the church or into separately constructed church houses. For those too old or infirm to stand for long periods a stone ledge was sometimes provided along the nave wall for them to lean against.

The benches at Dunsfold in Surrey are reputed to be the earliest surviving examples in Britain, dating from the thirteenth or fourteenth century, but wooden benches did not appear in churches in any significant numbers until the latter half of the fifteenth century. The reason for their appearance is not entirely clear, as it did not coincide with any significant change

Spaxton, Somerset: many bench ends date from the time of the Reformation or after. Here the '5' of the date 1536 is made up of two fishes.

in ritual practice, but, although the sermon was not universally adopted as part of the service until the seventeenth century, there was a general tendency in the later middle ages for sermons to be preached by friars and this may have encouraged the introduction of church seating. In addition, the increased prosperity of parish communities in the later middle ages enabled them to rebuild their churches on a grand scale and, no doubt simultaneously, to desire greater comfort inside the church.

The overwhelming majority of surviving medieval benches are to be found in the West Country and East Anglia. The reason for this has never been satisfactorily explained, although it is these two areas whose churches contain the largest quantity of medieval woodwork generally. It has been argued that the introduction of church seating was a result of the prosperity derived from the wool trade. East Anglia and Somerset were among the leading areas for the production of woollen cloth in the later middle ages,

but Cornwall was not. In East Anglia good stone for building, let alone sculpture, was scarce, so the tradition of woodcarving was very strong there. To some extent this also applied in Cornwall, where the granite was not well suited for finely worked sculpture. However, in the Cotswolds and the East Riding (North Humberside), two of the most prosperous areas, stone carving was pre-eminent, and they have almost no medieval benches and no tradition of woodcarving.

Although the benches very often had carved backs and fronts, it was the bench ends that were the focus of attention. These were normally made from a single piece of oak up to 5 inches (127 mm) thick. There are two basic styles of bench end and they conform roughly to locality and date. The typical West Country bench end is sixteenth-century and is square-headed. Here the carving was applied in relief to the face of the bench end, except for a few examples in Cornwall, such as at Madron, where the subject matter was carved on the top.

8

Above: *Cossington, Leicestershire: in the Elizabethan era linenfold panelling became increasingly popular and marks the first move away from medieval style.*

Right: *Wiggenhall St Mary, Norfolk: here and at the neighbouring church of St Germans the bench ends, with their saints in niches and figures on arm rests, are the most sumptuously carved in Britain.*

The East Anglian benches date from the late fifteenth century onwards and have many minor variations in style. most have a finial, or poppy-head, at the top and a moulded arm rest with a figure carved on top. The face of the bench end could then have relief carving or be left plain. The earlier West Country bench ends, for example at East Brent and Rimpton in Somerset, also have poppy-heads, as do most of the pre-Reformation benches in other parts of Britain.

The bench ends featured in this book were all produced before 1600. Although this includes benches produced after the Reformation, when the Renaissance had brought in a new artistic style, most of the bench ends are still medieval in character. However, profile figures in Renaissance dress and the simple decorative motif of linenfold panelling became popular in the Elizabethan age.

9

Left: *Altarnun, Cornwall: the carver of this bench end chose a winged angel bearing a shield to display his name on his work. Unfortunately the date is now illegible.*

Right: *Broomfield, Somerset: the mis-spelt inscription by the carver Simon Werman. The style of edge moulding has been used to identify other works by the same carver.*

THE CARVERS AND THEIR WORK

We know very little about the individual craftsmen who produced the carvings. Most of what we do know comes from written records, which are generally more complete for abbey and cathedral churches than for parish churches. In a number of cases the name of a master carpenter is recorded, but he was not necessarily the person who carved the misericords. For example, at St George's Chapel, Windsor Castle, William Berkeley is recorded as the chief carver for the making of the stalls, but not all of the carvings are by the same hand. Parish records provide us

with a few names of individuals who were employed in the construction of benches. At Bodmin in Cornwall the churchwardens engaged Matthew More in 1491 to construct seats similar to those at Plympton, Devon, and a man named Glosse was sent from Stogursey in Somerset to Wales in 1524 to find 'bordes' suitable for benches.

There are no misericords on which the name of a carver has been inscribed, but in some cases the carver left his own personal mark. At Lincoln Cathedral the carver decorated the rim of the ledge with four-leaved flowers and at Bristol Cathedral one of the carvers incorporated what are meant either to be mice or rabbits into his work. However, two names of carvers are recorded on bench ends. At Altarnun in Cornwall a bench end is inscribed RObART DAYE MAKER OF THIS WORKE. At Broomfield in Somerset a bench end has the name SIIMON WERMAN, and at nearby Trull are two bench ends with the initials SW and a third with

the date 1560. Parish records have shown that Simon Werman lived at Bicknoller in Somerset; he was born about 1520 and died in 1585. The specific form of edge moulding he used can be seen on bench ends in a number of other Somerset churches and this is the clearest picture we have of a craftsman producing benches for a number of parish churches in a localised area.

While this may have been common

Above: *Ripon Cathedral: misericord: a winged angel with the date 1489. The second figure is a half-eight, a common way of writing four.*

Below: *Exeter Cathedral: this, the only African elephant on a British misericord, may have been copied from a drawing of the elephant given to Henry II by Louis IX of France in 1255.*

11

Left: *Lincoln Cathedral: misericord supporter: a woman hawking, representing either May or October in the Labours of the Months, copied from an illuminated calendar.*

Right: *Milverton, Somerset: bench end: Joshua and Caleb returning from the Promised Land, copied from the Biblia Pauperum.*

practice for seating in parish churches, there is no doubt that the majority of misericords were produced by craftsmen with a regional or even national reputation. A good example is William Lyngwode, who was sent from Norwich to Winchester Cathedral in 1308 to build the stalls. Another is the school of carvers at Ripon Minster under the master craftsman William Bromflet. The misericords at Ripon are dated 1489-94 and the work of his school can also be seen at Manchester Cathedral and at Beverley Minster, where the misericords are dated 1520-4. The misericords carved at Bridlington and Kirkstall Abbey have not survived.

The carvers were able to draw on a wide range of sources for the subject matter of their work. Until printed books became widely available in the fifteenth century, the carvers would have been able to copy scenes from stone sculpture, wall paintings and glass inside the church and to represent scenes from their own experience of everyday life. The carvers are unlikely to have had much direct access to valuable manuscript illuminations, but the monks doubtless communicated ideas from them to the carver, as we have evidence they did to the stonemasons at Canterbury Cathedral.

Of contemporary books and manuscripts, the bestiaries were among the main sources of ideas. These were based on the earlier moralising tales of the *Physiologus* (the standard medieval guide to 'science', which in turn was derived from the Roman author Pliny). They combined observations of animal characteristics and behaviour with allegorical tales and provided the carver with a wealth of exotic creatures, both real and imaginary, all of which had a moral tale to tell.

Medieval romances and folk tales also provided ready subject matter. These included the romance of Tristan and Iseult, Jack and the Beanstalk (scenes from which appear on misericords at New College Chapel in Oxford) and the beast-epic of Reynard the Fox. For scenes from everyday life the carvers could rely on their own experience or copy scenes from calendars. Calendars gave lists of saints and were often illustrated with secular scenes in the form of the Labours of the Months.

A block book printed in the Nether-lands at the end of the fifteenth century and entitled the *Biblia Pauperum* has been shown to be the source of Bible scenes carved on misericords at Ripon and elsewhere. Another instance amongst many, where the precise source of a carving can be identified is the misericord scenes of Courting and Rape at Westminster Abbey. These were copied from engravings by Albrecht Dürer published in about 1495.

THE SUBJECT MATTER

Nearly half of all misericords in Britain, and an even greater percentage of their supporters, are decorated with foliage. With bench ends, the most common form of decoration is either foliage or panelling, although a large proportion of benches have no decoration at all. Beyond this, the subject matter of the carvings is richly varied. In the iconography, or visual language, of medieval art it is often very difficult to distinguish religion from mythology and everyday life, as every aspect of earthly existence was interpreted as representing some aspect of God's will. The classification of subjects into groups here is a convenient way to describe them, but it should be recognised that such a classification is a modern rather than a medieval idea. Consequently many subjects do not fall neatly into categories.

RELIGIOUS SCENES

Carvings of religious scenes occur rarely on misericords. Perhaps their hidden location was too great a temptation for the carvers to resist indulging in more creative freedom than was possible elsewhere. It has also been suggested that the clergy would have thought it inappropriate to sit on sacred effigies of Christ, the Virgin Mary or the Apostles. Bench ends, however, being visible inside the nave of the church, could be very effective as didactic art, and it is this class of carvings which has the overwhelming majority of religious scenes.

The most common reference to an episode from the life of Christ is to the Passion. This was represented by a number of symbols associated with the Crucifixion such as a hammer, nails, pincers, a spear, a sponge and a ladder. The Five Wounds of Christ — hands, feet and heart — were also commonly represented. Passion symbols are found most often in Cornwall, although they appear to a lesser extent in all areas where bench ends are found. Their importance was in their association with prayers seeking pardon from sin, and the symbols themselves were copied from devotional woodcuts. Carvings depicting the Crucifixion itself are, by comparison, uncommon, and very few show the Nativity, Resurrection or Ascension, although the last is portrayed on a misericord at Lincoln Cathedral.

Scenes from the Old Testament offered a richer source of inspiration, particularly for misericord carvers, and it would appear that publication of the *Biblia Pauperum* in the late fifteenth century renewed interest in the subject. At Worcester and Ely cathedrals there are misericords showing the Temptation of Adam and Eve and their subsequent banishment from the Garden of Eden. Again at Worcester Cathedral there are misericords illustrating the lives of Isaac, Moses, Samson and Solomon. Other popular Old Testament stories include Jonah and the Whale, and the now less well known story of Joshua and Caleb, the spies of Eschol who returned from the

Left: *Launcells, Cornwall: the spear, sponge, nails and hammer are among the many Passion symbols on the bench ends in this church.*

Right: *Abbotsham, Devon: the Crucifixion. The figures of Saints Mary and John have been defaced, and the head in profile at the bottom is probably to commemorate the donor of the benches.*

Promised Land carrying a huge bunch of grapes.

Saints were revered in the medieval world because they symbolised a tangible link between earthly and divine existence. Each of the saints was depicted with his or her attribute, usually alluding to their martyrdom, which was how the saints could be identified. Thus St Andrew was portrayed with a saltire cross, St Laurence with a gridiron, and St Catherine with a wheel. The Four Evangelists, Matthew, Mark, Luke and John, had winged creatures as their emblems — an angel, a lion, an ox and an eagle respectively.

Alongside virtue, the vices also had their place. The Seven Deadly Sins — pride, covetousness, lust, anger, gluttony, sloth and envy — were portrayed on a number of bench ends in East Anglia, the most famous sets being at Blythburgh in Suffolk and Wiggenhall St Germans in Norfolk. However, the sins depicted, which at Blythburgh include drunkenness, do not always correspond to the capital sins of the theologians.

Carvings of liturgical subjects are rare, although rosaries appear on a number of bench ends and misericords, and a holy water vessel and sprinkler appear on a bench end at Milverton in Somerset. At

Above left: *Worcester Cathedral: misericord: Samson rending the lion's jaws, one of a number of scenes on the misericords here supposed to have been copied from paintings in the chapter house.*

Above right: *Wiggenhall St Mary, Norfolk: bench end: St Agatha, shown with her breast being cut off.*

Right: *Canon Pyon, Herefordshire: misericord of a wheel, symbol of St Catherine.*

Left: *Wiggenhall St Germans, Norfolk: bench end: St Jude, brother of St James the Less, with his attribute, a boat.*

Centre: *Wiggenhall St Germans, Norfolk: bench end: St John, holding a cup from which a serpent is emerging, referring to the attempt to poison him.*

Right: *Blythburgh, Suffolk: a bench-end finial showing a figure sitting up in bed, representing sloth, one of the Seven Deadly Sins.*

Trull in Somerset is a remarkable set of five bench ends showing a religious procession of an acolyte, crucifer, chorister, deacon and priest.

CREATURES OF THE IMAGINATION

These are creatures which were outside the carvers' own experience. Some of them are mythological, like the unicorn, mermaid and wyvern: others, like the tiger and elephant, were real but the carvers had never seen them. The elephant in the bestiaries and on misericords and bench ends is, with one notable exception, the Indian elephant. The legendary size of the animal was exaggerated until the howdah on its back became a castle — the origin of the familiar motif of the elephant and castle. The carvers were not interested in anatomical correctness here, nor in carvings of lions and tigers, most of which are wholly unconvincing in the naturalistic sense, but in the allegorical tales that were associated with them.

Far right: *Freck-enham, Suffolk: a bench-end finial showing the Devil pushing one of the damned into the jaws of Hell, a warning to unrepentant sinners.*

Near right: *Trent, Dorset: the first of four bench ends reading 'Ave Maria gratia plena Dominus tecum ame' (Hail Mary, full of grace, the Lord is with thee, Amen).*

Below: *Lakenheath, Suffolk: bench end: this creature can be identified as a tigress because she is looking into a mirror. Instead of paws the creature has been given hooves.*

17

Above: *Norwich Cathedral: misericord: a rare portrayal of a four-legged dragon. Note how the front leg becomes a wing and is not attached to the body.*

Left: *Ripon Cathedral: misericord supporter: a blemya, described by Pliny as a man with his facial features in his torso.*

The creatures were used to symbolise both virtues and vices. According to the bestiaries the elephant lived for three hundred years and bred only once. In order to mate, the female plucked a mandrake, which encouraged the hitherto passionless male to copulate — an allusion to Eve offering Adam the forbidden fruit. Its genitals being placed backwards, the elephant coupled back to back, thus enabling it to look away from the carnal act and preserve its virtue of modesty. The camel had the virtue of humility. It is portrayed in a stooped position (usually a symbol of adoration) principally because it needed to stoop to take up its burden, an allusion to Christ's humility and his acceptance of the burden of mankind.

The carvers seem most to have enjoyed the portrayal of animals that represented evil. Like the elephant, the tigress had a fanciful tale attached to it. A hunter who had stolen tiger cubs and was being pursued by the mother was to throw down a mirror in front of the tigress. The mother, seeing her own reflection, would be fooled into thinking it was one of her cubs in front of her and, in the words of a thirteenth-century Franciscan friar, 'is long occupied therefore to deliver the children out of the glass', allowing the hunter to escape. This story was used by preaching friars in the later middle ages to warn of the decoys which enable the Devil to steal away men's souls. The four-legged dragon and the much more popular two-legged wyvern were more direct representations of the Devil. The mermaid, which in pre-Christian mythology was a conveyor of souls to Hades, became in the bestiaries a seductress ready to steal away the souls of men, warning of the sin of copulation. The

Dennington, Suffolk: bench end: a sciapod, who, according to the bestiaries, lived in the desert and used his large foot to shade himself from the sun. Here the carver has mistakenly given him two feet.

19

St George's Chapel, Windsor Castle: a mermaid in her role as a seductress, holding a mirror and a comb. The left supporter is an ibis capturing an eel, the right an otter with a fish.

unicorn was a hunting creature who sought to lay his head in the lap of a virgin. He was, therefore, hunted by men and the method of capture was either to use a virgin as live bait or for the hunter to reveal himself to the unicorn and then duck behind a tree. The artless unicorn would then attack and get its horn stuck in the tree trunk. Both methods of capture were illustrated on misericords, but on bench ends the carvers more often portrayed the unicorn in an heraldic rather than an allegorical context.

Even when portraying animals which they knew the carvers would adopt the bestiary version. The pelican, for instance, was not shown in any naturalistic context, but always restoring her young to life by feeding them with her own blood. This was after having slain them for their rebelliousness, thus symbolising the Fall and Redemption of Mankind.

Greystoke, Cumbria: misericord: the hunter, on the left, has captured the unicorn by using a virgin as live bait.

Above: *Carlisle Cathedral: misericord: a bestiary hyena, with its legendary rigid spine, devouring a disinterred corpse.*

Right: *Crowcombe, Somerset: a Green Man with foliage emanating from his mouth and mermen emerging from his ears.*

Again the hyena was portrayed not for its own sake but because a hyena feeding on a disinterred corpse represented vice feeding on corruption.

Not all creatures of the imagination came from bestiary sources. The demon Tutivillus, whose role was to copy down the conversations between gossippers in church and then take them back to the Devil to be read out on the Day of Judgement, was a familiar figure from medieval morality plays. Another popular figure was the Green Man, a creature of apparently indigenous British pagan origin, who symbolised natural regeneration. He is usually shown with foliage growing out of his mouth, although at Exeter Cathedral he is shown wearing a satyr's mask with the foliage sprouting from his head.

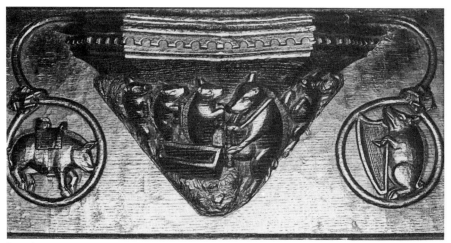

Beverley Minster, Humberside: a sow plays the bagpipes while the piglets dance. The supporters are a saddled pig on the left and a pig playing the harp on the right.

EVERYDAY LIFE

The craftsmen also produced a number of carvings of animals from their own experience, not all of which had a bestiary source. Woodpeckers, cranes, finches and herons were portrayed amongst foliage. Some of these, like the gyrfalcon on a misericord at Winchester College, were naturalistic but most had a symbolic context, like the geese falling prey to the fox. Several species of bat also occur on misericords and it has been argued that some were carved from freshly dead specimens. With its wings unfolded, a bat was an ideal shape for the carving of a misericord.

Apart from their religious and moral attributes, animals were also used for the portrayal of humour and satire. Reynard the Fox, captured, tried, then hanged by the geese, was used to satirise mendicant friars. The most popular animal for portraying humour was the pig, a motif which the Ripon school of carvers used to good effect. Thus we find pigs dancing and playing musical instruments, the sound of bagpipes being likened to the squealing of pigs. The hare riding a hound at Worcester and the rabbits roasting a hunter on a spit while boiling his hound in a large pot at Manchester are in the same humorous vein. They are all

designed to illustrate the world turned on its head, which appealed greatly to the medieval sense of humour. This theme was developed in a number of proverbs like 'shoeing the goose', a reference to cowboy tradesmen, a subject on a misericord at Beverley Minster. Apes also appear in a variety of guises, as a friend of Reynard the Fox or as a satire on the medical profession. Another theme that the celibate monks must have found especially amusing was the domestic brawl. These invariably show the woman pursuing the man, always victorious and often violent.

The misericord carvers could narrate the lives of medieval people by portraying the Ages of Man and the Labours of the Months. No complete sequence of the Ages of Man has survived, although it is sometimes difficult to establish whether some scenes refer to the Labours or the Ages. Childhood was represented by childish games — a hobby horse at Sherborne Abbey, handball at Gloucester Cathedral — and youth by a teacher birching a boy holding a book.

For the Labours of the Months the carvers were able to copy scenes from calendars and psalters, most of which were continental in origin. The publication in 1493 of a shepherd's calendar, *Le*

22

Beverley Minster, Humberside: a misericord illustrating the proverb of putting the cart before the horse. The 'cart' is in fact the earliest recorded reaping machine.

Cartmel Priory, Cumbria: misericord: an ape holding up a urine bottle, a satirical jibe at the little respected medical profession.

Fairford, Gloucestershire: misericord: domestic strife — a woman preparing to strike her husband with a ladle.

Lavenham, Suffolk: a female creature plays a viol while her male counterpart mocks her by drawing a crutch across a pair of bellows. This misericord in unusual in that it has no supporters.

Compost et Kalendrier des Bergiers, in Paris, seems to have revived interest in the subject. This continental origin meant that September is sometimes portrayed as the harvesting of grapes, which was not a significant event in the calendar of rural Britain. Conversely sheep shearing, the most important event in the year to the British farmer and the source of the nation's wealth, appears on only one misericord, at Beverley Minster.

The only complete set of the Labours of the Months is at Ripple in Worcestershire. In most cases the carvers simply copied one or two scenes, not necessarily in any particular order, and sometimes for the supporters rather than the main design. The scenes depicting each month varied, but usually there were scenes such as reaping corn in August, fattening pigs with acorns in October and slaughtering the pigs in November. At Ripple and Great Malvern January is represented symbolically by a man holding up two

Right: *St George's Chapel, Windsor Castle: misericord supporter: Death comes to the labourer, part of the only surviving Dance of Death sequence on a British misericord.*

Below: *Ripple, Worcestershire: misericord: reaping corn using a sickle and a wooden crook; August in the Labours of the Months.*

Above: *Ludlow, Shropshire: a man wrapped in a thick woollen costume warms himself by the fire, while two sides of bacon hang in the larder; one of the winter months in the Labours sequence.*

Below left: *Davidstow, Cornwall: bench end: a piper.*

Below right: *St Winnow, Cornwall: this ship records the importance of the sea to the livelihood of Cornish people.*

Above: *Manchester Cathedral: misericord: two men playing tric-trac, or backgammon. A woman on the right is drawing ale from a barrel. The woman on the left is supposed to be making pastry.*

Left: *St Levan, Cornwall: bench end: a jester wearing his fool's cap and bells. Note the wooden clogs.*

wine cups. This was derived from the two-headed Janus in Roman mythology, where one head looked back to the old year, the other forward to the new.

The bench-end carvers relied much more on their own experiences for illustrating everyday life and here we see all aspects of work and play. Carvings illustrating the woollen industry are few in number, although shepherds, a fuller and his tools, shuttles and cloth shears appear in various places. Other carvings showing the trades and professions include ale tasters, millers (and windmills) and, at Ixworth Thorpe in Suffolk, a thatcher with his rake and knife. People at play were also popular, especially in hunting scenes, which appeared in the Labours of the Months and occur frequently on misericords. In Cornwall there are bench ends in a number of churches showing entertainers like musicians, jesters, contortionists and sword dancers. Other

Left: *Ely Cathedral: misericord: a wrestling match. Note the oddly formed feet with their ridiculously long toes.*

Below: *Monkleigh, Devon: a coat of arms of an unknown family who must have donated the money for constructing the benches in the church.*

forms of entertainment like wrestling and cock fighting are also recorded.

The choir stalls, and especially the seating in parish churches, were often paid for by a single donor or by several together and the gift was commemorated among the carvings. In a number of churches in north Devon the initials of the various donors were carved on the bench ends, as likely as not backwards or upside down (probably because the carvers were illiterate). If the donor family had a coat of arms then this was the proper form of acknowledgement. Carvings also sometimes commemorate the king and the abbot or bishop. The foremost example of the former is in St George's Chapel, Windsor Castle, where Edward IV is shown meeting Louis XI of France, a meeting which took place in France in 1475 to discuss peace terms in the Hundred Years War. But this is an exception and the most popular royal motif was the Tudor rose. The armoured knights which appear on misericords remind us of the feudal system of the middle ages and many of these figures, like the legendary Swan Knight, allude to the Crusades.

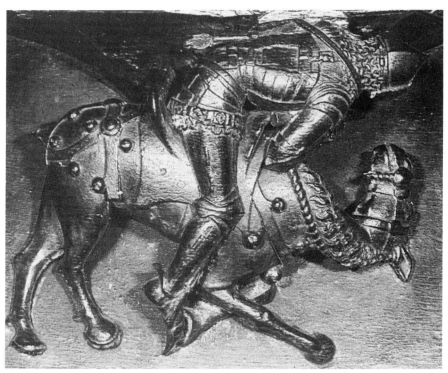

Lincoln Cathedral: misericord: an armoured knight with a crossbow bolt in his back falls from his horse.

THE REFORMATION AND AFTER

After the Dissolution of the Monasteries from 1536 to 1539 and the subsequent reorganisation of Christian ritual under Edward VI and Elizabeth I, misericords no longer had any practical function. Some of the former abbeys and collegiate churches became cathedrals or parish churches; others were abandoned. As they were destroyed or left to fall into ruin their misericords were almost always lost, although some were moved to neighbouring parish churches to be used as priests' stalls.

Misericords escaped relatively unscathed from the iconoclasm, or destruction of images, under Edward VI in 1550 and the Puritanism of the mid seventeenth century, although the Puritans destroyed the misericords at Canterbury Cathedral. A number of other factors, not least dry rot and woodboring insects, have contributed to the losses of misericords. The Great Fire of 1666 destroyed an incalculable number of misericords in London churches, but tradition has it that the misericords at Bishop's Stortford, Hertfordshire, are those salvaged from the ruins of St Paul's. All but two of the misericords from York Minster were destroyed in the fire there in 1829, and the Luftwaffe accounted for misericords in St Michael's Cathedral in Coventry.

Some of the more prudish Victorian clergy ordered misericords which they considered to be obscene or improper to be destroyed, as happened at Chester Cathedral. At St Nicholas, King's Lynn, a carpenter was ordered to destroy all the misericords he had removed from the chancel. Luckily, in this case, they eventually found their way to the Victoria and Albert Museum. Wilful destruction of this kind apparently continued until the early years of the twentieth century.

Bench ends have had a very different history since the middle ages. The preaching of sermons became universal in the seventeenth century and all parish churches would have been wholly or partly furnished with seating by this time. The Puritan inconoclasts did little damage to bench ends beyond disfiguring images of saints and the most serious losses of bench-end carvings occurred in the eighteenth and nineteenth centuries.

One reason for this was doubtless the decay of old woodwork. Another was the introduction of box pews in the eighteenth century. These were designed to keep out draughts and were more comfortable than their medieval counterparts. So medieval benches were removed, a practice that continued into the nineteenth century, especially in town churches, which were often heavily restored and refurnished. Given the enthusiasm of the Victorians for medieval art and architecture, it is, perhaps, surprising that they removed so much medieval woodwork and replaced it with plain deal benches. However, in their defence, they were responsible for repairing a good number of bench ends that had been damaged by dry rot and in many cases they incorporated bench-end panels into pulpits, screens and choir stalls when they were removed. Even so, the losses of bench ends have been considerable and they have even been seen incorporated into farmhouse and vicarage furniture. One authority on the subject even found a bench end by the carver Simon Werman for sale in an antique shop.

Churchstanton, Somerset: when box pews were introduced into this church in the early nineteenth century the medieval bench ends were re-used for the facade of a gallery.

PLACES TO VISIT

The following county lists include misericords and bench ends in cathedrals, churches and chapels. For counties rich in bench ends the list is more selective than for other counties. The letter M in brackets after the place-name indicates misericords, while B denotes bench ends. Other places of interest not included here may be found by consulting Sir Nikolaus Pevsner's *Buildings of England* and G. L. Remnant's *Catalogue of Misericords in Great Britain* (see 'Further reading').

ENGLAND

Avon. Berkeley Castle (M). Bristol Cathedral (M). Churchill (B). Weston-in-Gordano (M). Worle (M).
Bedfordshire. Bedford (M). Leighton Buzzard (M). Northill (M). Stevington (B). Swineshead (M).
Berkshire. Windsor Castle, St George's Chapel (M).
Buckinghamshire. Aylesbury (M). Edlesborough (M). North Marston (M).
Cambridgeshire. Balsham (M). Cambridge: Jesus College Chapel (M); King's College Chapel (M); Pembroke College Chapel (M); St John's College Chapel (M). Coveney (B). Ely Cathedral (M). Fordham (M). Godmanchester (M). Ickleton (B). Isleham (B, M). Orwell (M). Over (M). St Neots (M). Soham (M). Swaffham Bulbeck (B). Swavesey (B).
Cheshire. Chester Cathedral (M). Malpas (M). Nantwich (M).
Cornwall. Altarnun (B). Davidstow (B). Gorran (B). Kilkhampton (B). Lansallos (B). Launcells (B). Madron (B). Mullion (B). Padstow (M). St Buryan (M). St Columb Major (B). St Levan (B). St Winnow (B). Zennor (B).
Cumbria. Carlisle Cathedral (M). Cartmel Priory (M). Greystoke (M).
Derbyshire. Bakewell (M). Church Gresley (M). Hartshorne (B). Tideswell (M).
Devon. Abbotsham (B). Atherington (M). Braunton (B). Colebrooke (B). Combeinteignhead (B). Down St Mary (B). East Budleigh (B). Exeter Cathedral (M). Frithelstock (B). High Bickington (B). Landcross (B). Lewtrenchard (B). Monkleigh (B). Ottery St Mary (M). Yarcombe (B).
Dorset. Affpuddle (B). Bradford Abbas (B). Christchurch Priory (M). Hilfield (B). Milton Abbas (B). Sherborne Abbey (M). Trent (B). Wimborne Minster (M). Yetminster (B).
Durham. Bishop Auckland: St Andrew (M); Castle Chapel (M). Brancepeth (M). Darlington (M). Durham: Cathedral (M); Castle Chapel (M). Lanchester (M). Sedgefield (M). Staindrop (M).
East Sussex. Etchingham (M).
Essex. Belchamp (M). Castle Hedingham (M). Wendens Ambo (B).

Gloucestershire. Buckland (B). Duntisbourne Rous (M). Fairford (M). Gloucester Cathedral (M). Tewkesbury Abbey (M).
Greater London. Beddington (M). Stepney, Royal Foundation of St Catherine (M). Victoria and Albert Museum (M). Westminster Abbey, Henry VII's Chapel (M).
Greater Manchester. Manchester Cathedral (M). Middleton (M).
Hampshire. Alton (M). Amport (B). Winchester: Cathedral (M); College Chapel (M).
Hereford and Worcester. Canon Pyon (M). Great Malvern, Priory (M). Harvington (B). Hereford: All Saints (M); Cathedral (M); St Peter (M). Holme Lacy (M). Ledbury (M). Leintwardine (M). Madley (M). Moccas (M). Ripple (M). Worcester Cathedral (M).
Hertfordshire. Anstey (M). Ashwell (B). Bishop's Stortford (M). Stevenage (M).
Humberside. Beverley: Minster (M); St Mary (M). Swine (M).
Kent. Aldington (M). Ashford (M). East Barming (B). Faversham (M). Herne (M). Lenham (M). Maidstone (M). Minster in Thanet (M). Wingham (M).
Lancashire. Blackburn Cathedral (M). Garstang (M). Halsall (M). Lancaster Priory (M). Whalley (M).
Leicestershire. Ab Kettleby (B). Cossington (B). Croxton Kerrial (B). Misterton (B). Thornton (B).
Lincolnshire. Boston (M). Lincoln Cathedral (M). Osbournby (B). Walcot (B). Wigtoft (B).
Merseyside. Bebington (M). Prescot (M). Sefton (M). Woodchurch (B).
Norfolk. Ashmanhaugh (B). Cley (B). Feltwell (B). Gooderstone (B). Hockham (B). King's Lynn, St Margaret (M). Norwich Cathedral (M). Salle (M). Thornham (B). Thurgarton (B). Tilney (M). Upper Sheringham (B). Wiggenhall St Germans (B). Wiggenhall St Mary (B). Wilton (B).
Northamptonshire. Gayton (M). Hargrave (B). Hemington (M). Higham Ferrers (M). Holdenby (M). Irthlingborough (M). Lowick (B). Passenham (M). Rothwell (M). Tansor (M). Warkworth (B).
Northumberland. Hexham Abbey (M).
North Yorkshire. Hackness (M). Old Malton (M). Richmond (M). Ripon Cathedral (M).
Nottinghamshire. Newark (M). Nottingham, St Stephen (M). Sneiton (M). Southwell Minster (M). Thurgarton Priory (M). Wysall (M).
Oxfordshire. Hampton Poyle (B). Kidlington (B). Oxford: All Souls College Chapel (M); Lincoln College Chapel (M); Magdalen College Chapel (M); New College Chapel (M). Sutton Courtenay (M). Swinbrook (M). Wantage (M).
Shropshire. Ludlow (M). Tong (M).
Somerset. Barwick (B). Bishop's Lydeard (B). Brent Knoll (B). Broomfield (B). Crowcombe

31

(B). East Brent (B). East Quantoxhead (B). Hatch Beauchamp (B). Kingston (B). Lyng (B). Milverton (B). Spaxton (B). Trull (B). Wells Cathedral (M). **Staffordshire.** Clifton Campville (M). Enville (M). Farewell (M). Penkridge (M). **Suffolk.** Blythburgh (B). Dennington (B). Freckenham (B). Fressingfield (B). Honington (B). Ixworth Thorpe (B). Lakenheath (B). Lavenham (M). Norton (M). Southwold (M). Stowlangtoft (B, M). Sudbury (M). Wilby (B). Wingfield (M). Withersfield (B). Woolpit (B). Wordwell (B). **Surrey.** Dunsfold (B). Gatton (B). Lingfield (M). **Warwickshire.** Astley (M). Stratford-upon-Avon (M). **West Midlands.** Coventry, Holy Trinity (M). Knowle (M). Walsall (M). **West Sussex.** Arundel Castle, Fitzalan Chapel (M). Broadwater (M). Chichester: Cathedral (M); St Mary's Hospital (M). Climping (B).

East Lavant (M). West Tarring (M). **West Yorkshire.** Darrington (M). Halifax (M). Wakefield Cathedral (M). **Wiltshire.** Crudwell (B). Mere (M). Salisbury: Cathedral (M); St Thomas of Canterbury (M).

WALES
Clwyd. Gresford (M). St Asaph Cathedral (M). **Dyfed.** Haverfordwest (B). St David's Cathedral (M). **Gwent.** Abergavenny (M). **Gwynedd.** Abererch (M). Beaumaris (M). Clynnog (M). **Powys.** Brecon, Christ College Chapel (M). Montgomery (M).

SCOTLAND
Central. Dunblane Cathedral (M). **Grampian.** Aberdeen, King's College Chapel (M). **Lothian.** Edinburgh, National Museum of Antiquities of Scotland (M).

FURTHER READING

Anderson, M. D. *Misericords.* Penguin, 1954.
Anderson, M. D. *Imagery of British Churches.* John Murray, 1955.
Cox, J. C., and Harvey, A. *English Church Furniture.* EP Publishing, 1973.
Kraus, D. and H. *The Hidden World of Misericords.* Braziller, New York, 1975.
Laird, Marshall. *English Misericords.* John Murray, 1986.
Remnant, G. L. *A Catalogue of Misericords in Great Britain.* Clarendon Press, 1969.
Smith, J. C. D. *A Guide to Church Woodcarvings.* David and Charles, 1974.